Classic Wisdom

— FOR THE —

GOOD
LIFE

CLASSIC WISDOM

— FOR THE —

GOOD LIFE

EDITED BY

BRYAN CURTIS

THOMAS NELSON
Since 1798

NASHVILLE DALLAS MEXICO CITY RIO DE JANEIRO BEIJING

Published in Nashville, Tennessee, by Thomas Nelson. Thomas Nelson is a trademark of Thomas Nelson, Inc.

Thomas Nelson, Inc. titles may be purchased in bulk for educational, business, fund-raising, or sales promotional use. For information, please e-mail SpecialMarkets@ThomasNelson.com.

Design by Stacy Clark

Library of Congress Cataloging-in-Publication

Classic wisdom for the good life / edited by Bryan Curtis.
    p. cm.
  ISBN 13: 978-1-4016-0303-8 (hard cover)
  ISBN 13: 978-1-4016-0305-2 (leather)
  1. Conduct of life—Quotations, maxims, etc. I. Curtis, Bryan.
  PN6084.C556C46 2006
  170'.44—dc22

                        2006007882

Printed in the United States of America

08 09 10 11 WOR 9 8 7 6 5 4

To Paige

The Good Life

It is what we all want for ourselves and those we love. But what exactly is the good life?

For some the good life means having a powerful job and living in a house so big no human can clean it without a staff of help. For others it means a healthy family and enough money to help others. But the good life does not encompass only one aspect of your life. A good life is a healthy mix of home and work and friends and fun.

This book celebrates excellence and provides wisdom from many sources from many different times. It is my hope that some of these words help or inspire or motivate you to achieve a life you deserve and of which you can be proud.

Many of the quotes in this book are specific about work or character or courage or achieving your dreams. But others are more subjective and can be applied to different aspects of your life. What most of them accomplish is to remind you that your destiny and your happiness are in your own hands.

So find one quote or 101 quotes that move you. Use them to make your life better. Use them to define and achieve the good life.

CLASSIC WISDOM

— FOR THE —

GOOD
LIFE

the
good
life

There are only two options regarding commitment. You're either in or out. There's no such thing as a life in-between.

—Pat Riley

Real integrity is doing the right thing, knowing that nobody's going to know whether you did it or not.

—Oprah Winfrey

The way to get started is to quit talking and begin doing.

—Walt Disney

You know, I used to think the future was solid or fixed, something you inherited like an old building that you move into when the previous generation moves out or gets chased out. But it's not. The future is not fixed; it's fluid. You can build your own building, or hut or condo . . . the world is more malleable than you think and it's waiting for you to hammer it into shape.

—BONO

The important thing is not to stop questioning. Curiosity has its own reason for existing. One cannot help but be in awe when he contemplates the mysteries of eternity, of life, of the marvelous structure of reality. It is enough if one tries merely to comprehend a little of this mystery every day. Never lose a holy curiosity.

—ALBERT EINSTEIN

College is something you complete. Life is something you experience. So don't worry about your grade, or the results or success. Success is defined in myriad ways, and you will find it, and people will no longer be grading you, but it will come from your own internal sense of decency.

—Jon Stewart

Waste your money and you're only out of money, but waste your time and you've lost a part of your life.

—Michael LeBoeuf

Labor disgraces no man, but occasionally men disgrace labor.

—Ulysses S. Grant

Hold fast to dreams, for if dreams die, life is
a broken, winged bird that cannot fly.

—LANGSTON HUGHES

You will, undoubtedly, meet people
who will try to shut you up or entice
you to compromise your principles
in any number of ways. They'll try to
seduce you and distract you with
money, power, security and
perhaps, most dangerously, a sense
of belonging. Don't let them; it's
just not worth it.

—SAMUEL L. JACKSON

An invincible determination can
accomplish almost anything, and in
this lies the great distinction between
great men and little men.

—THOMAS FULLER

Ask yourself: Have you been kind today?
Make kindness your daily modus operandi
and change your world.

—Annie Lennox

I have yet to find the man, however exalted his station, who did not do better work and put forth greater effort under a spirit of approval than under a spirit of criticism.

—CHARLES SCHWAB

▪ ▪ ▪ ▪ ▪ ▪ ▪

When the heart is right, the mind and the body will follow.

—CORETTA SCOTT KING

When you give yourself the gift of quietly believing in yourself, you'll love yourself. And now for another tip. It is of paramount importance for you to figure out as soon as possible that you must do things that make you love yourself. I'm sure you've all heard the line, "If you don't first love yourself, you can never truly love anyone else." Well, that's true. No one in the world can solve the problems of one who does not love herself, and you can spend years thinking that if someone could just love me the right way, then everything will be okay. And that's true, it's just that that someone is you. Because I know so well how easy it is to be hard on yourself, too hard, and how unforgiving one can be when it comes to one's own shortcomings. And of course, some healthy self-criticism is good, but I also know how negative voices inside you can get carried away, until that's all you hear.

—CALLIE KHOURI

When one door closes another door opens;

but we so often look so long and so

regretfully upon the closed door, that we

do not see the ones which open for us.

—ALEXANDER GRAHAM BELL

The man who has no imagination
has no wings.

—Muhammad Ali

It's not what you look at that matters,
it's what you see.

—Henry David Thoreau

A man may die, nations may rise
and fall, but an idea lives on.

—John F. Kennedy

It's easy to make a buck. It's a lot
tougher to make a difference.

—Tom Brokaw

Draw strength from the knowledge that education will break the backs of poverty, disenfranchisement, and violence; that war is never inevitable but only a terrible failure of the imagination; and that love is stronger than hatred.

—WALLY LAMB

■ ■ ■ ■ ■ ■ ■ ■

Never confuse a single defeat with a final defeat.

—F. SCOTT FITZGERALD

To be successful, this **education** must foster the habit of critical thinking, rooting out the inconsistencies of self-serving ethical thought; this suggests a key role for religious and secular philosophy. And it must also **nourish** the **imagination;** this suggests a key role for the arts. Third, it must offer much more **knowledge** of the world: the major world religions, economic conditions in developing countries, the deprivations with which a large proportion of the world's people **live** from day to day.

—MARTHA C. NUSSBAUM

Achievement of your happiness is the only moral purpose of your life, and that happiness, not pain or mindless self-indulgence, is the proof of your moral integrity, since it is the proof and the result of your loyalty to the achievement of your values.

—AYN RAND

A winner is someone who recognizes his God-given talents, works his tail off to develop them into skills, and uses these skills to accomplish his goals.

—LARRY BIRD

I submit to you that if a man hasn't discovered something that he will die for, he isn't fit to live.

—MARTIN LUTHER KING JR.

To finish first, you must first finish.

—RICK MEARS

Even if you are on the right track, you

will get run over if you just sit there.

—WILL ROGERS

We plant seeds that will flower as results
in our lives, so best to remove the weeds
of anger, avarice, envy and doubt,
that peace and abundance may
manifest for all.

—DOROTHY DAY

■ ■ ■ ■ ■ ■ ■ ■

A positive attitude may not solve
all your problems, but it will annoy
enough people to make it worth
the effort.

—HERM ALBRIGHT

■ ■ ■ ■ ■ ■ ■ ■

Of course, you can't gain ground
if you are standing still.

—BILL CLINTON

A leader, once convinced a particular course of action is the right one, must have the determination to stick with it and be undaunted when the going gets rough.

—RONALD REAGAN

Don't be too timid and squeamish about your actions. All life is an experiment. The more experiments you make the better.

—RALPH WALDO EMERSON

Ninety-nine percent of the failures come from people who have the habit of making excuses.

—GEORGE WASHINGTON

■ ■ ■ ■ ■ ■ ■ ■

Education is a social process. Education is growth. Education is not a preparation for life; education is life itself.

—JOHN DEWEY

■ ■ ■ ■ ■ ■ ■ ■

In matters of principle, stand like a rock; in matters of taste, swim with the current.

—THOMAS JEFFERSON

If you want anything to actually change or to move ahead in your life you actually have to do it yourself, you can't sit there and wait for somebody or talk about what you might want . . . you should actually keep dreams and desires inside and let them burn a little bit, and then they might come true.

—Russell Crowe

Good people are good because they've come to wisdom through failure.

—WILLIAM SAROYAN

■ ■ ■ ■ ■ ■ ■ ■

The person who makes a success of living is the one who sees his goal steadily and aims for it unswervingly. That is dedication.

—CECIL B. DEMILLE

■ ■ ■ ■ ■ ■ ■ ■

I believe the destiny of your generation— and your nation—is a rendezvous with excellence.

—LYNDON B. JOHNSON

Millions of men have lived to fight, build palaces and boundaries, shape destinies and societies; but the compelling force of all times has been the force of originality and creation profoundly affecting the roots of human spirit.

—ANSEL ADAMS

■ ■ ■ ■ ■ ■ ■ ■

Continue to expose yourself to new ideas. Trust your instincts and think for yourself. Make art, or at least value it.

—SAMUEL L. JACKSON

You don't have to be a "person of influence" to be influential. In fact, the most influential people in my life are probably not even aware of the things they've taught me.

—SCOTT ADAMS

The only completely consistent people are the dead.

—ALDOUS HUXLEY

■ ■ ■ ■ ■ ■ ■ ■

Efforts and courage are not
enough without purpose
and direction.

—JOHN F. KENNEDY

■ ■ ■ ■ ■ ■ ■ ■

Difference of opinion leads to enquiry,
and enquiry to truth.

—THOMAS JEFFERSON

Desire is the key to motivation, but it's determination and commitment to an unrelenting pursuit of your goal—a commitment to excellence—that will enable you to attain the success you seek.

—MARIO ANDRETTI

But I, being poor, have only my dreams; I have spread my dreams under your feet; tread softly because you tread on my dreams.

—W. B. YEATS

Genius is one percent inspiration and
ninety-nine percent perspiration.

—Thomas A. Edison

Ability is what you're capable of
doing. Motivation determines
what you do. Attitude determines
how well you do it.

—Lou Holtz

Never work just for money or for power.
They won't save your soul or help
you sleep at night.

—Marian Wright Edelman

I know the price of success: dedication,

hard work, and an unremitting devotion

to the things you want to see happen.

—FRANK LLOYD WRIGHT

He has a right to criticize,
who has a heart to help.

—ABRAHAM LINCOLN

Always be smarter than
the people who hire you.

—LENA HORNE

Work for something because
it is good, not just because it
stands a chance to succeed.

—VÁCLAV HAVEL

Honesty is the first chapter
in the book of wisdom.

—THOMAS JEFFERSON

I don't wait for moods. You
accomplish nothing if you do that.
Your mind must know it has got to
get down to work.

—PEARL S. BUCK

■ ■ ■ ■ ■ ■ ■ ■

Confidence . . . thrives on honesty,
on honor, on the sacredness of
obligations, on faithful protection and
on unselfish performance. Without
them it cannot live.

—FRANKLIN D. ROOSEVELT

■ ■ ■ ■ ■ ■ ■ ■

Dreams are the touchstones
of our characters.

—HENRY DAVID THOREAU

The future turns out to be something that you make instead of find. It isn't waiting for your arrival, either with an arrest warrant or a band, nor is it any further away than the next sentence, the next best guess, the next sketch for the painting of a life portrait that might become a masterpiece. The future is an empty canvas or a blank sheet of paper, and if you have the courage of your own thought and your own observation, you can make of it what you will.

—LEWIS LAPHAM

Facts are stubborn things; and whatever
may be our wishes, our inclinations, or the
dictates of our passions, they cannot alter
the state of facts and evidence.

—John Adams

Achievement is largely the product
of steadily raising one's levels of
aspiration . . . and expectation.

—Jack Nicklaus

Start by doing what's necessary,
then what's possible, and suddenly you
are doing the impossible.

—St. Francis of Assisi

Respect a man, and he will
do all the more.

—John Wooden

Always give your best, never get

discouraged, never be petty; always

remember, others may hate you.

Those who hate you don't win

unless you hate them. And then

you destroy yourself.

—RICHARD M. NIXON

If you don't have enemies, you
don't have character.

—PAUL NEWMAN

The foolish and the dead alone never
change their opinion.

—JAMES RUSSELL LOWELL

There are one hundred men
seeking security to one able man
who is willing to risk his fortune.

—J. PAUL GETTY

Imagination has brought mankind through the dark ages to its present state of civilization. Imagination led Columbus to discover America. Imagination led Franklin to discover electricity.

—L. Frank Baum

■ ■ ■ ■ ■ ■ ■ ■

Those of us who govern can sometimes inspire, and we can identify needs and marshal resources, but we simply cannot be the managers of everything and everybody.

—Jimmy Carter

When things go wrong
don't go with them.

—Elvis Presley

■ ■ ■ ■ ■ ■ ■ ■

You must capture and keep the heart
of the original and supremely able man
before his brain can do its best.

—Andrew Carnegie

■ ■ ■ ■ ■ ■ ■ ■

The past is but the beginning
of a beginning.

—H. G. Wells

From now on, any definition of a successful

life must include serving others.

—GEORGE H. W. BUSH

■ ■ ■ ■ ■ ■ ■ ■

Do you know the difference between

education and experience? Education is

when you read the fine print; experience is

what you get when you don't.

—PETE SEEGER

Wisdom doesn't automatically come with old age. Nothing does—except wrinkles. It's true, some wines improve with age. But only if the grapes were good in the first place.

—ABIGAIL VAN BUREN

■ ■ ■ ■ ■ ■ ■ ■

To put the world right in order, we must first put the nation in order; to put the nation in order, we must first put the family in order; to put the family in order, we must first cultivate our personal life; we must first set our hearts right.

—CONFUCIUS

The human mind is our
fundamental resource.

—John F. Kennedy

■ ■ ■ ■ ■ ■ ■ ■

Sooner or later, those who win are those
who think they can.

—Richard Bach

■ ■ ■ ■ ■ ■ ■ ■

My heroes are the ones who
survived doing it wrong, who
made mistakes, but recovered
from them.

—Bono

Nothing in this world can take the place of persistence. Talent will not; nothing is more common than unsuccessful people with talent. Genius will not; un-rewarded genius is almost a proverb.

—CALVIN COOLIDGE

■ ■ ■ ■ ■ ■ ■ ■

A strong nation, like a strong person, can afford to be gentle, firm, thoughtful, and restrained. It can afford to extend a helping hand to others. It's a weak nation, like a weak person, that must behave with bluster and boasting and rashness and other signs of insecurity.

—JIMMY CARTER

The greatest discovery of our generation is that human beings can alter their lives by altering their attitudes of mind. As you think, so shall you be.

—WILLIAM JAMES

■ ■ ■ ■ ■ ■ ■

A desire to be observed, considered, esteemed, praised, be loved and admired by his fellows is one of the earliest as well as the keenest dispositions discovered in the heart of a man.

—JOHN ADAMS

One of my superstitions had always

been when I started to go anywhere,

or to do anything, not to turn back,

or stop until the thing intended

was accomplished.

—Ulysses S. Grant

How wonderful it is that nobody need wait a single moment before starting to improve the world.

—Anne Frank

The only man who never makes a mistake is the man who never does anything.

—Theodore Roosevelt

Never apologize for showing feeling. When you do so, you apologize for the truth.

—Benjamin Disraeli

I am very little inclined on any occasion to say anything unless I hope to produce some good by it.

—Abraham Lincoln

So many of our dreams at first
seem impossible, then they seem
improbable, and then, when we
summon the will, they soon
become inevitable.

—CHRISTOPHER REEVE

An honorable defeat is better than
a dishonorable victory.

—MILLARD FILLMORE

Through pride we are ever
deceiving ourselves. But deep
down below the surface of
the average conscience a still,
small voice says to us,
"Something is out of tune."

—CARL JUNG

Nearly all men can stand adversity,
but if you want to test a man's
character, give him power.

—ABRAHAM LINCOLN

Courage without conscience
is a wild beast.

—ROBERT G. INGERSOLL

Be courteous to all, but intimate with few,
and let those few be well tried before you
give them your confidence.

—GEORGE WASHINGTON

Surround yourself with the best
people you can find, delegate
authority, and don't interfere.

—RONALD REAGAN

Clothes and manners do not make the man;
but when he is made, they greatly
improve his appearance.

—ARTHUR ASHE

I think we all have a little voice inside

us that will guide us. It may be God, I don't

know. But I think that if we shut out all the

noise and clutter from our lives and

listen to that voice, it will tell us the

right thing to do.

—CHRISTOPHER REEVE

A good heart is better than all the heads in the world.

—EDWARD BULWER-LYTTON

■ ■ ■ ■ ■ ■ ■ ■

Creativity is allowing yourself to make mistakes. Art is knowing which ones to keep.

—SCOTT ADAMS

■ ■ ■ ■ ■ ■ ■ ■

There is no point at which you can say, "Well, I'm successful now. I might as well take a nap."

—CARRIE FISHER

The most important single ingredient in the formula of success is knowing how to get along with people.

—THEODORE ROOSEVELT

■ ■ ■ ■ ■ ■ ■ ■

When you are in any contest, you should work as if there were—to the very last minute—a chance to lose it. This is battle. This is politics. This is anything.

—DWIGHT D. EISENHOWER

The true measure of a man is how
he treats someone who can do
him absolutely no good.

—Samuel Johnson

■ ■ ■ ■ ■ ■ ■ ■

Take time to deliberate; but when the time
for action arrives, stop thinking and go in.

—Andrew Jackson

■ ■ ■ ■ ■ ■ ■ ■

Only if you have been in the
deepest valley can you ever know
how magnificent it is to be on the
highest mountain.

—Richard M. Nixon

A man's character is like a tree and his reputation like its shadow; the shadow is what we think of it; the tree is the real thing.

—Abraham Lincoln

■ ■ ■ ■ ■ ■ ■ ■

The right thing to do never requires any subterfuge; it is always simple and direct.

—Calvin Coolidge

Everybody pities the weak;
jealousy you have to earn.

—ARNOLD SCHWARZENEGGER

You can't operate a company by fear,
because the way to eliminate fear is to
avoid criticism. And the way to avoid
criticism is to do nothing.

—STEVE ROSS

To love oneself is the beginning of a
lifelong romance.

—OSCAR WILDE

Your **time** is limited, so don't waste it living someone else's **life.** Don't be trapped by dogma—which is living with the results of other people's thinking. Don't let the noise of others' opinions drown out your own **inner voice.** And most important, have the courage to follow your **heart** and **intuition.** They somehow already know what you truly want to become. **Everything** else is secondary.

—STEVE JOBS

If everything seems under control,
you're just not going fast enough.

—Mario Andretti

Obstacles are those frightful things you see
when you take your eyes off your goal.

—Henry Ford

Labor to keep alive in your breast
that little spark of celestial fire
called conscience.

—George Washington

People ask the difference in a leader and a
boss. The leader leads and the boss drives.

—Theodore Roosevelt

And while the law of competition may

be sometimes hard for the individual,

it is best for the race, because it

ensures the survival of the fittest

in every department.

—ANDREW CARNEGIE

If you work just for money, you'll never make it, but if you love what you're doing and you always put the customer first, success will be yours.

—RAY ARTHUR KROC

■ ■ ■ ■ ■ ■ ■ ■

That's all a man can hope for during his lifetime—to set an example— and when he is dead, to be an inspiration for history.

—WILLIAM MCKINLEY

You've got to get to the stage in life where going for it is more important than winning or losing.

—ARTHUR ASHE

▪ ▪ ▪ ▪ ▪ ▪ ▪ ▪

Anytime you see a turtle up on top of a fence post, you know he had some help.

—ALEX HALEY

▪ ▪ ▪ ▪ ▪ ▪ ▪ ▪

If you do build a great experience, customers tell each other about that. Word of mouth is very powerful.

—JEFF BEZOS

Listen with an open heart and an open mind to those who love you the most. You may hear a grain of truth that will later become the foundation of your entire belief system.

—CALLIE KHOURI

■ ■ ■ ■ ■ ■ ■ ■

Hard work spotlights the character of people: some turn up their sleeves, some turn up their noses, and some don't turn up at all.

—SAM EWING

■ ■ ■ ■ ■ ■ ■ ■

America, at its best, matches a commitment to principle with a concern for civility. A civil society demands from each of us good will and respect, fair dealing and forgiveness.

—GEORGE W. BUSH

Either you deal with what is the reality, or you can be sure that the reality is going to deal with you.

—ALEX HALEY

■ ■ ■ ■ ■ ■ ■ ■

No race can prosper till it learns that there is as much dignity in tilling a field as in writing a poem.

—BOOKER T. WASHINGTON

■ ■ ■ ■ ■ ■ ■ ■

Mistakes are the portals of discovery.

—JAMES JOYCE

I've come to believe that each of us has a
personal calling that's as unique as a
fingerprint and that the best way to
succeed is to discover what you love and
then find a way to offer it to others in the
form of service, working hard, and
also allowing the energy of the
universe to lead you.

—OPRAH WINFREY

Self-respect is the fruit of
discipline; the sense of dignity
grows with the ability to say
no to oneself.

—ABRAHAM HESCHEL

Courage is what it takes to stand up and
speak; courage is also what it takes
to sit down and listen.

—WINSTON CHURCHILL

Education's purpose is to replace
an empty mind with an open one.

—MALCOLM FORBES

Take a method and try it. If it fails,
admit it frankly, and try another. But by all
means, try something.

—FRANKLIN D. ROOSEVELT

If you have made mistakes, even serious ones, there is always another chance for you. What we call failure is not the falling down, but the staying down.

—Mary Pickford

■ ■ ■ ■ ■ ■ ■ ■

It is a paradoxical but profoundly true and important principle of life that the most likely way to reach a goal is to be aiming not at that goal itself but at some more ambitious goal beyond it.

—Arnold Toynbee

One man with courage
makes a majority.

—ANDREW JACKSON

Work is not a curse; it is the prerogative of
intelligence, the only means of manhood,
and the measure of civilization.

—CALVIN COOLIDGE

A goal without a plan
is just a wish.

—ANTOINE DE SAINT-EXUPERY

You can't wait for inspiration. You have to go after it with a club.

—Jack London

Fight for your opinions, but do not believe that they contain the whole truth, or the only truth.

—Charles A. Dana

I think a hero is an ordinary individual who finds strength to persevere and endure in spite of overwhelming obstacles.

—Christopher Reeve

Let us think of education as the means

of developing our greatest abilities,

because in each of us there is a private

hope and dream which, fulfilled,

can be translated into benefit for

everyone and greater strength

for our nation.

—JOHN F. KENNEDY

It's a damn poor mind that can think of
only one way to spell a word.

—ANDREW JACKSON

Few things are impossible to
diligence and skill. Great works
are performed not by strength,
but perseverance.

—SAMUEL JOHNSON

Energy and persistence conquer all things.

—BENJAMIN FRANKLIN

I believe that one of life's greatest
risks is never daring to risk.

—OPRAH WINFREY

■ ■ ■ ■ ■ ■ ■ ■ ■

Accomplishments will prove to be

a journey, not a destination.

—DWIGHT D. EISENHOWER

You can't build a reputation on
what you are going to do.

—HENRY FORD

Hide not your talents,
they for use were made.
What's a sun-dial in the shade?

—BENJAMIN FRANKLIN

You have to have confidence in
your ability, and then be tough
enough to follow through.

—ROSALYNN CARTER

Far better to think historically, to remember the lessons of the past. Thus, far better to conceive of power as consisting in part of the knowledge of when not to use all the power you have. Far better to be one who knows that if you reserve the power not to use all your power, you will lead others far more successfully and well.

—A. Bartlett Giamatti

■ ■ ■ ■ ■ ■ ■ ■

Success, the real success, does not depend upon the position you hold but upon how you carry yourself in that position.

—Theodore Roosevelt

There is no pleasure in having
nothing to do; the fun is having
lots to do and not doing it.

—ANDREW JACKSON

People of mediocre ability sometimes
achieve outstanding success because they
don't know when to quit. Most men
succeed because they are determined to.

—GEORGE ALLEN

Duty is ours; results are God's.

—JOHN QUINCY ADAMS

The test of a first-rate intelligence is the ability to hold two opposed ideas in mind at the same time and still retain the ability to function.

—F. Scott Fitzgerald

■ ■ ■ ■ ■ ■ ■ ■

It is the duty of a citizen not only to observe the law, but to let it be known that he is opposed to its violation.

—Calvin Coolidge

The only true disability in life is
a bad attitude.

—Scott Hamilton

■ ■ ■ ■ ■ ■ ■ ■

You make a living by what you get,
you make a life by what you give.

—Winston Churchill

■ ■ ■ ■ ■ ■ ■ ■

Victory has a thousand fathers but
defeat is an orphan.

—John F. Kennedy

In preparing for battle, I have always
found that plans are useless, but planning
is indispensable.

—Dwight D. Eisenhower

■ ■ ■ ■ ■ ■ ■ ■

Are you bored with life? Then
throw yourself into some work you
believe in with all your heart, live
for it, die for it, and you will find
happiness that you had thought
could never be yours.

—Audrey Hepburn

■ ■ ■ ■ ■ ■ ■ ■

If you're not failing every now and again,
it's a sign you're not doing anything
very innovative.

—WOODY ALLEN

So whatever you plan to do, whether you plan to travel the world next year, go to graduate school, join the workforce, or take some time off to think, don't just listen to your head. Listen to your heart. It's the best career counselor there is. Do what you really love to do and if you don't know quite what that is yet, well, keep searching, because if you find it, you'll bring that something extra to your work that will help ensure you will not be automated or outsourced. It will help make you an untouchable radiologist, an untouchable engineer, or an untouchable teacher.

—THOMAS L. FRIEDMAN

I have never considered a difference of opinion in politics, in religion, in philosophy, as a cause for withdrawing from a friendship.

—THOMAS JEFFERSON

■ ■ ■ ■ ■ ■ ■

No man is justified in doing evil on the ground of expediency.

—THEODORE ROOSEVELT

■ ■ ■ ■ ■ ■ ■

If you don't get noticed, you don't have anything. You just have to be noticed, but the art is in getting noticed naturally, without screaming or without tricks.

—LEO BURNETT

I would rather lose in a cause that will someday win, than win in a cause that will someday lose.

—Woodrow Wilson

■ ■ ■ ■ ■ ■ ■ ■

Life's most urgent question is: what are you doing for others?

—Martin Luther King Jr.

Freedom lies in being bold.

—ROBERT FROST

■ ■ ■ ■ ■ ■ ■ ■

There are no such things as limits to growth,
because there are no limits on the
human capacity for intelligence,
imagination and wonder.

—RONALD REAGAN

■ ■ ■ ■ ■ ■ ■ ■

Don't be fooled by the calendar.
There are only as many days in the
year as you make use of.

—CHARLES RICHARDS

Dream as if you'll live forever.
Live as if you'll die today.

—JAMES DEAN

■ ■ ■ ■ ■ ■ ■ ■

It's a mere moment in a man's life
between an All-Star Game and an
Old-timers' Game.

—VIN SCULLY

You have enemies? Good. That means

you've stood up for something,

sometime in your life.

—WINSTON CHURCHILL

Courage is being afraid
but going on anyhow.

—DAN RATHER

It's not hard to make decisions when
you know what your values are.

—ROY DISNEY

The hardest thing to learn in life is
which bridge to cross and which to burn.

—DAVID RUSSELL

Far and away the best prize that life
has to offer is the chance to work hard
at work worth doing.

—THEODORE ROOSEVELT

It may be those who do most,
dream most.

—STEPHEN LEACOCK

■ ■ ■ ■ ■ ■ ■ ■

Leadership is action, not position.

—DONALD H. MCGANNON

■ ■ ■ ■ ■ ■ ■ ■

The impossible is often
the untried.

—JIM GOODWIN

Use power to help people. For we are given power not to advance our own purposes, nor to make a great show in the world, nor a name. There is but one just use of power and it is to serve people.

—GEORGE H. W. BUSH

■ ■ ■ ■ ■ ■ ■ ■

Some men see things as they are and say why—I dream things that never were and say why not.

—GEORGE BERNARD SHAW

To be a success in business,
be daring, be first, be different.

—HENRY MARCHANT

Life brings sorrows and joys alike.
It is what a man does with them—
not what they do to him—that is
the true test of his mettle.

—THEODORE ROOSEVELT

A man's reputation is the opinion people
have of him; his character is
what he really is.

—JACK MINER

Champions aren't made in gyms.
Champions are made from something
they have deep inside them—a desire,
a dream, a vision. They have to have
last-minute stamina, they have to be
a little faster, they have to have the
skill and the will. But the will must
be stronger than the skill.

—MUHAMMAD ALI

A man is known by the company he keeps, and also by the company from which he is kept out.

—Grover Cleveland

▪ ▪ ▪ ▪ ▪ ▪ ▪ ▪

I think you should take your job seriously, but not yourself—that is the best combination.

—Judi Dench

Delay is preferable to error.

—Thomas Jefferson

■ ■ ■ ■ ■ ■ ■ ■

People ask for your criticism, but they only want your praise.

—W. Somerset Maugham

■ ■ ■ ■ ■ ■ ■ ■

The man who is swimming against the stream knows the strength of it.

—Woodrow Wilson

Talent is what you possess; genius
is what possesses you.

—MALCOLM COWLEY

There is no indispensable man.

—WOODROW WILSON

Bravery is being the only one
who knows you're afraid.

—FRANKLIN P. JONES

Man is still the most extraordinary
computer of all.

—JOHN F. KENNEDY

Embrace the **faith** that every challenge

surmounted by your energy; every problem

solved by your **wisdom;** every soul

stirred by your **passion;** and every

barrier to justice brought down by your

determination will ennoble your

own life, inspire others, serve your country,

and explode outward the boundaries of

what is **achievable** on this earth.

—MADELEINE ALBRIGHT

First, make yourself a reputation
for being a creative genius. Second,
surround yourself with partners who are
better than you are. Third, leave
them to get on with it.

—David Ogilvy

▪ ▪ ▪ ▪ ▪ ▪ ▪ ▪

The best executive is one who has
sense enough to pick good people to
do what he wants done, and self-
restraint enough to keep from meddling
with them while they do it.

—Theodore Roosevelt

Do not bite the bait of pleasure
till you know there is no hook
beneath it.

—THOMAS JEFFERSON

■ ■ ■ ■ ■ ■ ■ ■

A pound of pluck is worth a
ton of luck.

—JAMES A. GARFIELD

■ ■ ■ ■ ■ ■ ■ ■

Greatness lies not in being strong,
but in the right use of strength.

—HENRY WARD BEECHER

Never underestimate the power of dreams and the influence of the human spirit. We are all the same in this notion. The potential for greatness lives within each of us.

—WILMA RUDOLPH

I believe, with abiding conviction, that this people—nurtured by their deep faith, tutored by their hard lessons, moved by their high aspirations—have the will to meet the trials that these times impose.

—LYNDON B. JOHNSON

One of the greatest victories you can gain over someone is to beat him at politeness.

—Josh Billings

■ ■ ■ ■ ■ ■ ■ ■

You never have trouble
if you are prepared for it.

—Theodore Roosevelt

■ ■ ■ ■ ■ ■ ■ ■

An expert is a person who has made all the mistakes that can be made in a very narrow field.

—Niels Bohr

Let us have faith that right
makes might.

—Abraham Lincoln

One cool judgment is worth a thousand
hasty counsels. The thing to be supplied is
light, not heat.

—Woodrow Wilson

Trying to be someone else is a
waste of the person you are!

—Kurt Cobain

If you can't stand the heat,
get out of the kitchen.

—Harry S. Truman

Risk! Risk anything! Care no more for the

opinions of others, for those voices. Do the

hardest thing on earth for you. Act for

yourself. Face the truth.

—Katherine Mansfield

GOOD

Never forget that it is the spirit with

which you endow your work that

makes it useful or futile.

—ADELAIDE HASSE

Tolerance implies no lack of commitment to one's beliefs. Rather it condemns the oppression or persecution of others.

—JOHN F. KENNEDY

■ ■ ■ ■ ■ ■ ■ ■

Never let a problem to be solved become more important than the person to be loved.

—BARBARA JOHNSON

■ ■ ■ ■ ■ ■ ■ ■

Ideas are like stars; you will not succeed in touching them with your hands. But like the seafaring man on the desert of waters, you choose them as your guides, and following them you will reach your destiny.

—CARL SCHURZ

And as for the final sphere of love and friendship, I can only say it gets harder once the natural communities of college and hometown are gone . . . . It takes work and commitment, demands toleration for human frailties, forgiveness for the inevitable disappointment and betrayals that come even with the best of relationships.

—DORIS KEARNS GOODWIN

Patience is the companion of wisdom.

—Saint Augustine

■ ■ ■ ■ ■ ■ ■ ■

Aim for success, not perfection. Never give up your right to be wrong, because then you will lose the ability to learn new things and move forward with your life.

—David M. Burns

■ ■ ■ ■ ■ ■ ■ ■

It is easier to do a job right than to explain why you didn't.

—Martin Van Buren

Inspiration is wonderful when it happens,
but the writer must develop an approach for
the rest of the time . . . The wait is simply
too long.

—LEONARD BERNSTEIN

■ ■ ■ ■ ■ ■ ■ ■

Happiness depends more
upon the internal frame of a
person's own mind, than on the
externals in the world.

—GEORGE WASHINGTON

■ ■ ■ ■ ■ ■ ■ ■

Never interrupt your enemy when he is
making a mistake.

—NAPOLEON BONAPARTE

What convinces is conviction. Believe in

the argument you're advancing. If you

don't, you're as good as dead. The other

person will sense that something isn't there,

and no chain of reasoning, no matter

how logical or elegant or brilliant,

will win your case for you.

—LYNDON B. JOHNSON

Many of life's failures are people who did
not realize how close they were to success
when they gave up.

—THOMAS A. EDISON

■ ■ ■ ■ ■ ■ ■ ■

Take calculated risks. That is quite
different from being rash.

—GEORGE S. PATTON

■ ■ ■ ■ ■ ■ ■ ■

Don't expect to build up the weak by
pulling down the strong.

—CALVIN COOLIDGE

Turn your wounds
into wisdom.

—Oprah Winfrey

Leaders must invoke an
alchemy of great vision.

—Henry Kissinger

It is amazing what you can accomplish if you do not care who gets the credit.

—HARRY S. TRUMAN

■ ■ ■ ■ ■ ■ ■ ■

The stories of past courage . . . can teach, they can offer hope, they can provide inspiration. But they cannot supply courage itself. For this each man must look into his own soul.

—JOHN F. KENNEDY

■ ■ ■ ■ ■ ■ ■ ■

Imagination will often carry us to worlds that never were. But without it we go nowhere.

—CARL SAGAN

Ultimately, the only power to which man should aspire is that which he exercises over himself.

—ELIE WIESEL

■ ■ ■ ■ ■ ■ ■ ■

The first man gets the oyster, the second man gets the shell.

—ANDREW CARNEGIE

Trust that little voice in your head
that says "Wouldn't it be interesting if . . ."
And then do it.

—Duane Michals

To educate a man in mind and
not in morals is to educate a
menace to society.

—Theodore Roosevelt

Wisdom is knowing what to do next;
virtue is doing it.

—David Starr Jordan

A noble man compares and estimates himself by an idea which is higher than himself; and a mean man, by one lower than himself. The one produces aspiration; the other ambition, which is the way in which a vulgar man aspires.

—MARCUS AURELIUS

■ ■ ■ ■ ■ ■ ■ ■

Wisdom is the reward you get for a lifetime of listening when you'd have preferred to talk.

—DOUG LARSON

I do not enter into agreements but with an intention of fulfilling them, and I expect the same punctuality on the part of those with whom they are made.

—GEORGE WASHINGTON

If you fear making anyone mad, then you ultimately probe for the lowest common denominator of human achievement.

—JIMMY CARTER

Success is how high you bounce
when you hit bottom.

—George S. Patton

◼ ◼ ◼ ◼ ◼ ◼ ◼ ◼

The most rewarding things you do in
life are often the ones that look like they
cannot be done.

—Arnold Palmer

◼ ◼ ◼ ◼ ◼ ◼ ◼ ◼

Justice and goodwill will
outlast passion.

—James A. Garfield

Your most unhappy customers are
your greatest source of learning.

—BILL GATES

Unless he has been part of a cause greater
than himself, no man is truly whole.

—RICHARD M. NIXON

A man without ambition is dead.
A man with ambition but no
love is dead.

—PEARL BAILEY

Ideas control the world.

—JAMES A. GARFIELD

I have found no greater satisfaction than achieving success through honest dealing and strict adherence to the view that, for you to gain, those you deal with should gain as well.

—ALAN GREENSPAN

If you're trying to achieve, there will be roadblocks. I've had them; everybody has had them. But obstacles don't have to stop you. If you run into a wall, don't turn around and give up. Figure out how to climb it, go through it, or work around it.

—MICHAEL JORDAN

America, at its best, is a place where personal responsibility is valued and expected.

—George W. Bush

■ ■ ■ ■ ■ ■ ■ ■

Nothing will work unless you do.

—Maya Angelou

■ ■ ■ ■ ■ ■ ■ ■

The wisest men follow their own direction.

—Euripides

We do not need to burn down
the house to kill the rats.

—HERBERT HOOVER

■ ■ ■ ■ ■ ■ ■ ■

Weak minds sink under
prosperity as well as adversity;
but strong and deep ones have
two high tides.

—DAVID HARE

■ ■ ■ ■ ■ ■ ■ ■

Pride costs more than hunger,
thirst and cold.

—THOMAS JEFFERSON

Be honest, and remember that honesty counts for nothing unless back of it lie courage and efficiency.

—THEODORE ROOSEVELT

■ ■ ■ ■ ■ ■ ■ ■

No person is your friend who demands your silence or denies your right to grow.

—ALICE WALKER

You'll never find a better sparring
partner than adversity.

—Golda Meir

Leadership: the art of getting someone
else to do something you want done
because he wants to do it.

—Dwight D. Eisenhower

Victory belongs to the
most persevering.

—Napoleon Bonaparte

A man does what he must—in spite of
personal consequences, in spite of obstacles
and dangers and pressures—and that is
the basis of all human morality.

—John F. Kennedy

A man who views the world the same at fifty as he did at twenty has wasted thirty years of his life.

—MUHAMMAD ALI

To err is nature—to rectify error is glory.

—GEORGE WASHINGTON

The truth always turns out to be simpler
than you thought.

—Richard Feynman

The price of greatness is responsibility.

—Winston Churchill

So as you figure out the kind of work **you** want to do, the challenge is to find work imbued with **meaning,** work that provides **enjoyment** on a daily basis. If you choose a career for money or prestige or security but dislike going to work more days than not, it will never be worth it in the long run. As for the sphere of play, I've **learned** over the years that even with sports and recreation and hobbies, there's a need for a level of commitment of **time** and **energy** deep enough to really enjoy something and be able to derive relaxation from it.

—DORIS KEARNS GOODWIN

He who rejects change is the architect of decay. The only human institution which rejects progress is the cemetery.

—EDMUND WILSON

■ ■ ■ ■ ■ ■ ■ ■

I would never read a book if it were possible for me to talk half an hour with the man who wrote it.

—WOODROW WILSON

Confidence is contagious. So is lack of confidence.

—Vince Lombardi

■ ■ ■ ■ ■ ■ ■ ■

To be one, to be united is a great thing. But to respect the right to be different is maybe even greater.

—Bono

■ ■ ■ ■ ■ ■ ■ ■

Put a grain of boldness into everything you do.

—Baltasar Gracian

Don't follow any advice, no matter how good, until you feel as deeply in your spirit as you think in your mind that the counsel is wise.

—JOAN RIVERS

■ ■ ■ ■ ■ ■ ■ ■

Nothing can stop the man with the right mental attitude from achieving his goal; nothing on earth can help the man with the wrong mental attitude.

—THOMAS JEFFERSON

Forgiveness is a virtue
of the brave.

—INDIRA GANDHI

Measure iniquity by the heart, whether
a man's purse be full or empty, partly full or
partly empty. If the man is a decent man,
whether well off or not well off, stand by
him; if he is not a decent man, stand
against him, whether he be rich or poor.

—THEODORE ROOSEVELT

A man is not finished when
he is defeated. He is finished
when he quits.

—RICHARD M. NIXON

Modesty is a virtue that can never thrive in public. . . . A man must be his own trumpeter. He must get his picture drawn, his statue made, and must hire all the artists in his turn, to set about the works to spread his name, make the mob stare and gape, and perpetuate his fame.

—JOHN ADAMS

The recipe for perpetual ignorance is: be satisfied with your opinions and content with your knowledge.

—ELBERT HUBBARD

You may be disappointed if you
fail, but you are doomed
if you don't try.

—Beverly Sills

Associate yourself with men of good quality
if you esteem your own reputation, for 'tis
better to be alone than in bad company.

—George Washington

We did not invent human rights. In
a very real sense . . . human rights
invented America.

—Jimmy Carter

Creativity is the ability to introduce
order into the randomness
of nature.

—Eric Hoffer

The worst fear is the fear of living.

—Theodore Roosevelt

If your success is not on your own
terms, if it looks good to the world
but does not feel good in your
heart, it is not success at all.

—Anna Quindlen

No public man can be just a little crooked.
There is no such thing as a no-man's land
between honesty and dishonesty.

—Herbert Hoover

Fires can't be made with dead embers, nor can enthusiasm be stirred by spiritless men. Enthusiasm in our daily work lightens effort and turns even labor into pleasant tasks.

—James Baldwin

He who permits himself to tell a lie once, finds it much easier to do it a second and third time, till at length it becomes habitual; he tells lies without attending to it, and truths without the world's believing him. This falsehood of the tongue leads to that of the heart, and in time depraves all its good dispositions.

—Thomas Jefferson

Be practical as well as generous in your ideals. Keep your eyes on the stars, but remember to keep your feet on the ground.

—THEODORE ROOSEVELT

Our problems are man-made; therefore they may be solved by man. No problem of human destiny is beyond human beings.

—JOHN F. KENNEDY

It's hard to detect good luck—it looks so much like something you've earned.

—FRANK A. CLARK

If more politicians knew poetry, and more poets knew politics, I am convinced the world would be a little better place in which to live.

—JOHN F. KENNEDY

■ ■ ■ ■ ■ ■ ■ ■

Forgiveness is the economy of the heart . . . forgiveness saves the expense of anger, the cost of hatred, the waste of spirits.

—HANNAH MORE

What counts is not necessarily the size of the dog in the fight—it's the size of the fight in the dog.

—Dwight D. Eisenhower

■ ■ ■ ■ ■ ■ ■ ■ ■

Speak when you are angry—and you will make the best speech you'll ever regret.

—Laurence Peter

■ ■ ■ ■ ■ ■ ■ ■

It is neither wealth nor splendor, but tranquility and occupation, that gives happiness.

—Thomas Jefferson

Patience will achieve more than force.

—EDMUND BURKE

■　■　■　■　■　■　■　■

I cannot be intimidated from doing that

which my judgment and conscience tell me

is right by any earthly power.

—ANDREW JACKSON

Any man worth his salt will stick

up for what he believes is right, but

it takes a slightly better man to

acknowledge instantly and without

reservation that he is in error.

—ANDREW JACKSON

We grow great by dreams. All great men are dreamers.

—Woodrow Wilson

Success usually comes to those who are too busy to be looking for it.

—Henry David Thoreau

You live longer once you realize that any time spent being unhappy is wasted.

—Ruth E. Renkl

Stand with anybody that stands right. Stand with him while he is right, and part with him when he goes wrong.

—Abraham Lincoln

We cannot do great deeds unless we are willing to do the small things that make up the sum of greatness.

—THEODORE ROOSEVELT

■ ■ ■ ■ ■ ■ ■ ■

Leaders aren't born, they are made. And they are made just like anything else, through hard work. And that's the price we'll have to pay to achieve that goal, or any goal.

—VINCE LOMBARDI

Be wary of the man who urges an action in which he himself incurs no risk.

—Joaquin Setanti

■ ■ ■ ■ ■ ■ ■ ■

The best morale exists when you never hear the word mentioned. When you hear a lot of talk about it, it's usually lousy.

—Dwight D. Eisenhower

■ ■ ■ ■ ■ ■ ■ ■

Encouraging responsibility is not a search for scapegoats; it is a call to conscience. And though it requires sacrifice, it brings a deeper fulfillment.

—George W. Bush

It is not men that interest or disturb me primarily; it is ideas. Ideas live; men die.

—Woodrow Wilson

■ ■ ■ ■ ■ ■ ■ ■

The greater our knowledge increases, the more our ignorance unfolds.

—John F. Kennedy

■ ■ ■ ■ ■ ■ ■ ■

The dictionary is the only place that success comes before work. Hard work is the price we must pay for success. I think you can accomplish anything if you're willing to pay the price.

—Vince Lombardi

Take a stand for what's right. Raise a ruckus and make a change. You may not always be popular, but you'll be part of something larger and bigger and greater than yourself. Besides, making history is extremely cool.

—SAMUEL L. JACKSON

Dollars and guns are no substitutes for
brains and willpower.

—Dwight D. Eisenhower

Things do not change; we change.

—Henry David Thoreau

Conformity is the jailer of freedom
and the enemy of growth.

—John F. Kennedy

No person was ever honored for
what he received. Honor has been
the reward for what he gave.

—Calvin Coolidge

You gain strength, courage, and confidence by every experience in which you really stop to look fear in the face. You must do the thing which you think you cannot do.

—Eleanor Roosevelt

■ ■ ■ ■ ■ ■ ■ ■

The wisest thing to do with a fool is to encourage him to hire a hall and discourse to his fellow citizens. Nothing chills nonsense like exposure to air.

—Woodrow Wilson

Ability is sexless.

—Christabel Pankhurst

▪ ▪ ▪ ▪ ▪ ▪ ▪ ▪

My great concern is not whether you
have failed, but whether you are content
with your failure.

—Abraham Lincoln

▪ ▪ ▪ ▪ ▪ ▪ ▪ ▪

Morale is a state of mind. It is
steadfastness and courage and
hope. It is confidence and zeal and
loyalty. It is elan, ésprit de corps
and determination.

—George Marshall

I have not found this **generation** to be cynical or apathetic or selfish. They are as **strong** and as decent as any people that I have met. And I will say this, on my way down here I stopped at Bethesda Naval, and when you talk to the young kids that are there that have just been back from Iraq and Afghanistan, you don't have the worry about the **future** that you hear from so many that are not a part of this generation but judging it from **above.**

—JON STEWART

Nothing builds self-esteem and self-confidence like accomplishment.

—THOMAS CARLYLE

There is only one quality worse than hardness of heart and that is softness of head.

—THEODORE ROOSEVELT

Every child is an artist. The problem is how to remain an artist once he grows up.

—PABLO PICASSO

Don't compromise yourself. You are all you've got.

—JANIS JOPLIN

■ ■ ■ ■ ■ ■ ■ ■

Humility must always be the portion of any man who receives acclaim earned in blood of his followers and sacrifices of his friends.

—DWIGHT D. EISENHOWER

Success is a lousy teacher. It seduces smart people into thinking they can't lose.

—BILL GATES

The friend in my adversity I shall always cherish most. I can better trust those who helped to relieve the gloom of my dark hours than those who are so ready to enjoy with me the sunshine of my prosperity.

—ULYSSES S. GRANT

Knowledge will forever govern ignorance; and a people who mean to be their own governors must arm themselves with the power which knowledge gives.

—JAMES MADISON

The promise of America is a simple promise: Every person shall share in the blessings of this land. And they shall share on the basis of their merits as a person. They shall not be judged by their color, or by their beliefs, or by their religion, or by where they were born, or the neighborhood in which they live.

—LYNDON B. JOHNSON

■ ■ ■ ■ ■ ■ ■ ■

Luck is a dividend of sweat. The more you sweat, the luckier you get.

—RAY ARTHUR KROC

Poverty is uncomfortable; but nine times out of ten the best thing that can happen to a young man is to be tossed overboard and compelled to sink or swim.

—JAMES A. GARFIELD

■ ■ ■ ■ ■ ■ ■ ■

When written in Chinese, the word "crisis" is composed of two characters. One represents danger, and the other represents opportunity.

—JOHN F. KENNEDY

In any moment of decision, the best thing you can do is the right thing. The worst thing you can do is nothing.

—THEODORE ROOSEVELT

■ ■ ■ ■ ■ ■ ■ ■

My philosophy of life is that if we make up our mind what we are going to make of our lives, then work hard toward that goal, we never lose—somehow we win out.

—RONALD REAGAN

The first step to getting the things
you want out of life is this:
Decide what you want.

—BEN STEIN

The purpose of life is a life of purpose.

—ROBERT BYRNE

▪ ▪ ▪ ▪ ▪ ▪ ▪ ▪

Getting ahead in a difficult profession requires avid faith in yourself. That is why some people with mediocre talent, but with great inner drive, go much further than people with vastly superior talent.

—SOPHIA LOREN

▪ ▪ ▪ ▪ ▪ ▪ ▪ ▪

A hero is no braver than an ordinary man, but he is braver five minutes longer.

—RALPH WALDO EMERSON

When angry, count to ten before you speak. If very angry, a hundred.

—THOMAS JEFFERSON

Contrary to the cliché, genuinely nice guys most often finish first or very near it.

—MALCOLM FORBES

There are plenty of recommendations on how to get out of trouble cheaply and fast. Most of them come down to this: Deny your responsibility.

—LYNDON B. JOHNSON

To exclude from positions of **trust** and command all those below the age of 44 would have kept Jefferson from **writing** the Declaration of Independence, Washington from **commanding** the Continental Army, Madison from **fathering** the Constitution, Hamilton from **serving** as secretary of the treasury, Clay from being **elected** speaker of the House and Christopher Columbus from **discovering** America.

—JOHN F. KENNEDY

What you risk reveals
what you value.

—Jeanette Winterson

I would rather believe something and suffer
for it, than to slide along into success
without opinion.

—James A. Garfield

Actions speak louder than words.

—Theodore Roosevelt

America is successful because of the hard
work and creativity and enterprise of our
people. These were the true strengths of
our economy before September 11 and
they are our strengths today.

—George W. Bush

My motto was always to keep swinging.
Whether I was in a slump or feeling
badly or having trouble off the field, the
only thing to do was keep swinging.

—Hank Aaron

I would rather regret the things
that I have done than the things
that I have not.

—LUCILLE BALL

■ ■ ■ ■ ■ ■ ■ ■

Nothing gives one person so much
advantage over another as to remain always
cool and unruffled under all circumstances.

—THOMAS JEFFERSON

There are risks and costs to a program of action, but they are far less than the long-range risks and costs of comfortable inaction.

—JOHN F. KENNEDY

■ ■ ■ ■ ■ ■ ■ ■

All the extraordinary men I have known were extraordinary in their own estimation.

—WOODROW WILSON

Courtesy is as much a mark of
a gentleman as courage.

—Theodore Roosevelt

■ ■ ■ ■ ■ ■ ■ ■

Pull the string, and it will follow
wherever you wish. Push it, and it will
go nowhere at all.

—Dwight D. Eisenhower

■ ■ ■ ■ ■ ■ ■ ■

I am a great believer in luck,
and I find the harder I work,
the more I have of it.

—Thomas Jefferson

Help publicly. Help privately. Help in your actions by recycling and conserving and protecting, but help also in your **attitude.** Help make sense where sense has gone missing. Help bring **reason** and **respect** to discourse and debate. Help science to **solve** and faith to **soothe.** Help law bring justice, until justice is commonplace. Help and you will abolish apathy—the void that is so quickly filled by ignorance and evil.

—TOM HANKS

It is always better to be an original
than an imitation.

—THEODORE ROOSEVELT

■ ■ ■ ■ ■ ■ ■ ■

Create the highest, grandest vision
possible for your life because you
become what you believe.

—OPRAH WINFREY

■ ■ ■ ■ ■ ■ ■ ■

No one has a finer command of language
than the person who keeps his mouth shut.

—SAM RAYBURN

There is nothing worse than a brilliant image of a fuzzy concept.

—Ansel Adams

■ ■ ■ ■ ■ ■ ■ ■

America demands and deserves big things from us—and nothing big ever came from being small.

—Bill Clinton

Important principles may and must
be inflexible.

—ABRAHAM LINCOLN

It's kind of fun to do the impossible.

—WALT DISNEY

Character is a by-product; it is
produced in the great manufacture
of daily duty.

—WOODROW WILSON

Any jackass can kick down a barn, but it takes a good carpenter to build one.

—Lyndon B. Johnson

∎ ∎ ∎ ∎ ∎ ∎ ∎ ∎

Pride slays thanksgiving, but a humble mind is the soil out of which thanks naturally grow. A proud man is seldom a grateful man, for he never thinks he gets as much as he deserves.

—Henry Ward Beecher

If we focus our energies on sharing ideas,
finding solutions and using what is right with
America to remedy what is wrong with it,
we can make a difference. Our nation needs
bridges, and bridges are built by those who
look to the future and dedicate themselves
to helping others. I don't know what the
future holds, but I know who holds the
future: It is you.

—SANDRA DAY O'CONNOR

Tact is the ability to describe
others as they see themselves.

—ABRAHAM LINCOLN

* * * * * * * *

Of course there is no formula for success
except perhaps an unconditional
acceptance of life and what it brings.

—ARTHUR RUBINSTEIN

* * * * * * * *

I don't know the key to success,
but the key to failure is trying to
please everybody.

—BILL COSBY

What is right and what is practicable are two different things.

—JAMES BUCHANAN

■ ■ ■ ■ ■ ■ ■ ■

I am a slow walker, but I never walk back.

—ABRAHAM LINCOLN

■ ■ ■ ■ ■ ■ ■ ■

The influence of each human being on others in this life is a kind of immortality.

—JOHN QUINCY ADAMS

Things do not happen. Things are made to happen.

—JOHN F. KENNEDY

■ ■ ■ ■ ■ ■ ■

You'll make mistakes. Some people will call them failures but I have learned that failure is really God's way of saying, "Excuse me, you're moving in the wrong direction." It's just an experience, just an experience.

—OPRAH WINFREY

If wrinkles must be written upon our brows,
let them not be written upon the heart.
The spirit should not grow old.

—JAMES A. GARFIELD

■ ■ ■ ■ ■ ■ ■ ■

While I take inspiration from the
past, like most Americans,
I live for the future.

—RONALD REAGAN

■ ■ ■ ■ ■ ■ ■ ■

It is the American story—a story of flawed
and fallible people, united across the
generations by grand and enduring ideals.
The grandest of these ideals is an
unfolding American promise that everyone
belongs, that everyone deserves a
chance, that no insignificant
person was ever born.

—GEORGE W. BUSH

Twenty years from now you will be more disappointed by the things you didn't do than by the ones you did do. So throw off the bowlines. Sail away from the safe harbor. Catch the trade winds in your sails. Explore. Dream. Discover.

—MARK TWAIN

It takes a lot of courage to show your
dreams to someone else.

—ERMA BOMBECK

■ ■ ■ ■ ■ ■ ■ ■

So with imagination, ingenuity and
audacity, explore, discover, change the
world. And have fun while you're at it.
Always take time out to love and to live.
You're going to be busy, but never
forget family and friends.

—DANIEL S. GOLDIN

Old minds are like old horses: you must
exercise them if you wish to keep
them in working order.

—John Adams

When you see a rattlesnake poised
to strike you, do not wait until he
has struck before you crush him.

—Franklin D. Roosevelt

The most valuable of all talents is that of never using two words when one will do.

—THOMAS JEFFERSON

At the end of your life, you will never regret not having passed one more test, not winning one more verdict or not closing one more deal. You will regret time not spent with a husband, a child, a friend or a parent.

—BARBARA BUSH

Pessimism never won any battle.

—Dwight D. Eisenhower

■ ■ ■ ■ ■ ■ ■ ■

I am trying to do two things: dare to be a radical and not a fool, which is a matter of no small difficulty.

—James A. Garfield

■ ■ ■ ■ ■ ■ ■ ■

Happiness . . . it lies in the joy of achievement, in the thrill of creative effort.

—Franklin D. Roosevelt

There is one thing stronger than all
the armies in the world, and that is
an idea whose time has come.

—VICTOR HUGO

■ ■ ■ ■ ■ ■ ■ ■

And so, my fellow Americans: ask not what
your country can do for you—ask what you
can do for your country.

—JOHN F. KENNEDY

■ ■ ■ ■ ■ ■ ■ ■

When I give a man an office, I
watch him carefully to see whether
he is swelling or growing.

—WOODROW WILSON

Sooner or later we all discover that the important moments in life are not the advertised ones, not the birthdays, the graduations, the weddings, not the great goals achieved. The real milestones are less prepossessing. They come to the door of memory.

—SUSAN B. ANTHONY

Excellence demands competition. Without a race there can be no champion, no records broken, no excellence—in education or in any other walk of life.

—RONALD REAGAN

You are educated. Your certification is in

your degree. You may think of it as the

ticket to the good life. Let me ask you

to think of an alternative. Think of it

as your ticket to change the world.

—TOM BROKAW

Let us never negotiate out of fear. But let us never fear to negotiate.

—JOHN F. KENNEDY

A brave man is a man who dares to look the Devil in the face and tell him he is a Devil.

—JAMES A. GARFIELD

When you get an education, that is something nobody can take from you—money is only temporary—but what you have in your head, if you have the right kind of head, stays with you.

—HARRY S. TRUMAN

No man ever listened himself
out of a job.

—CALVIN COOLIDGE

■ ■ ■ ■ ■ ■ ■ ■

The time to repair the roof is when
the sun is shining.

—JOHN F. KENNEDY

■ ■ ■ ■ ■ ■ ■ ■

Whether you think you can or
think you can't, you're right.

—HENRY FORD

Faith is taking the first step even when you don't see the whole staircase.

—Martin Luther King, Jr.

■ ■ ■ ■ ■ ■ ■ ■

What's money? A man is a success if he gets up in the morning and goes to bed at night and in between does what he wants to do.

—Bob Dylan

A people that values its privileges
above its principles soon loses both.

—DWIGHT D. EISENHOWER

Get out of your way. You can spend
your life tripping on yourself; you can also
spend your life tripping yourself up. Get
out of your own way.

—SUZAN-LORI PARK

No one has the right to feel
hopeless, there's too much
work to do.

—DOROTHY DAY

Our lives improve only when we take
chances—and the first and most difficult risk
we can take is to be honest with ourselves.

—WALTER ANDERSON

Look, I don't want to wax philosophic, but I will say that if you're alive you've got to flap your arms and legs, you've got to jump around a lot, for life is the very opposite of death, and therefore you must at very least think noisy and colorfully, or you're not alive.

—MEL BROOKS

So what will define greatness for your generation? I believe it is to use the knowledge that you have earned here to find ways, not only to connect to computers, but to connect people; not only to bridge gaps in science, but to bridge gaps between cultures; not only to use numbers and formulas to create, but to use words to lead, and in the process, to close that canyon between ignorance and understanding.

—CARLY FIORINA

We have got but one life here. It pays, no matter what comes after it, to try and do things, to accomplish things in this life and not merely to have a soft and pleasant time.

—THEODORE ROOSEVELT

It takes tremendous discipline to control the influence, the power you have over other people's lives.

—CLINT EASTWOOD

The most important thing
about power is to make sure you
don't have to use it.

—EDWIN LAND

■ ■ ■ ■ ■ ■ ■ ■

God wants us to shake ourselves,
spread our pinions, and then lift
off and soar and rise, and rise
toward the confident and the good
and the beautiful. Rise towards the
compassionate and the gentle and the
caring. Rise to become what God
intends us to be—eagles,
not chickens.

—DESMOND TUTU

No one should negotiate their dreams.

Dreams must be free to fly high. No

government, no legislature, has a right

to limit your dreams. You should never

agree to surrender your dreams.

—JESSE JACKSON

The problems of the world cannot possibly be solved by skeptics or cynics whose horizons are limited by the obvious realities. We need men who can dream of things that never were.

—JOHN F. KENNEDY

Far better it is to dare mighty things, to win glorious triumphs, even though checkered by failure, than to take rank with those poor spirits who neither enjoy much nor suffer much, because they live in the gray twilight that knows not victory nor defeat.

—THEODORE ROOSEVELT

An opera begins long before the curtain goes up and ends long after it has come down. It starts in my imagination, it becomes my life, and it stays part of my life long after I've left the opera house.

—MARIA CALLAS

■ ■ ■ ■ ■ ■ ■ ■

Begin somewhere. You cannot build a reputation on what you intend to do.

—LIZ SMITH